Peter F. Copeland

EVERYDAY DRESS OF THE AMERICAN COLONIAL PERIOD

Coloring Book

Dover Publications, Inc.
New York

For Emer

INTRODUCTION

Everyday dress in America of the 1770s was largely the same as that in England, where clothing for the American upper classes was often made up on order. Foreigners traveling in America often remarked that the Americans copied the latest European fashions and were as well-dressed as folk in London or Paris. There were, however, some exceptions. In parts of rural New York, old-style Dutch fashions were still seen. German influence was strong in parts of Pennsylvania, and Highland Scottish clothing was worn by people in parts of western Virginia and North Carolina. Religious sects such as the Quakers wore distinctive clothing. On the frontiers, Indian garments were adopted or copied by pioneer families and hunters. In South Carolina and Georgia, colonists adopted forms of dress compatible with the warm climate. Dress in rural areas was usually more rude and simple than in the towns where people were more fashion-conscious and where bolts of cloth, buttons and other embellishments were more available.

Among the working classes, a man might often be recognized as a waggoner, a sailor, a smith or a butcher by the distinctive appearance of his working dress. Working women did not wear the elegant hoopskirts and elaborate hairstyles that ladies of the upper class sported.

Eighteenth-century clothing, for rich and poor alike, was usually individually made; ready-made clothing purchased in shops was rare. Those garments for the upper classes that were made in America were fashioned by tailors; the clothing of the working classes was usually made at home by the women of the house. In rural areas, textiles were usually handspun.

Wigs were going out of style at this time, but many gentlemen still wore them, while others had their hair curled and powdered with white flour. Young dandies preferred to have their own hair curled and styled by a barber.

Blazing scarlet and orange, sky blue, yellow, purple, rich crimson and brilliant green were colors frequently used in the clothing of the upper classes. Conservative elderly gentlemen, however, favored dress that was "snuff-colored"—a warm medium brown with a bit of red in it. Edgings and bindings to buttonholes were often of silver or gold, although not so much in the 1770s as they had been twenty years earlier. Lovely flowered patterns were fashionable among ladies of the upper classes.

The colors of working-class dress were generally more sober and drab—brick reds, dark blues and browns. Shirts, linens and trousers were frequently made of coarse Osnaburg linen left in its natural color—a pale yellow-brown. Homespun cloth tended toward middle browns and warm grays. Striped coarse fabrics such as mattress ticking and checked linen, both with red or blue stripes on a white ground, were used in making skirts, vests, jackets, shirts, trousers and aprons.

Everyday Dress of the American Colonial Period was first published as a new work in 1975 under the title of *Everyday Dress of the American Revolution.*

International Standard Book Number: 0-486-23109-7

Manufactured in the United States of America
Dover Publications, Inc., 31 East 2nd Street, Mineola, N.Y. 11501

1. The LAMPLIGHTER wears a striped workman's jacket, a double-breasted waistcoat or vest, leather breeches and a short apron. At his waist he carries a bundle of lampwicks and scissors for trimming them. He totes his ladder and oil pot for filling the lamps.

2. The SAILING MASTER was a warrant officer and navigator aboard ship. Naval officers usually wore uniforms, but seamen did not; warrant officers are usually depicted in seamen's dress. He wears a sailor's jacket, kerchief, a small cocked hat and petticoat trousers—short full trousers coming to just below the knee, made of coarse linen or old, worn sail canvas. The trousers were a protective garment; breeches worn underneath them were kept clean during work on deck.

3. The BROOM SELLER was a peddler who cried his wares through the streets of town. He wears a workman's jacket, a small round felt hat and breeches of mattress ticking.

4. The young HOUSE SERVANT is a slave dressed in livery—clothing in the colors of the family whom he serves. Black servants often wore turbans which, people felt, lent them a romantic African appearance. House servants in slavery were often forced to wear silver collars engraved with their owner's name.

5. The SHEPHERD wears a broad-brimmed felt hat for protection against the elements. A long surtout or watch coat, a farmer's shirt of coarse linen and leather breeches comprise his outfit. About his ankles he wears short gaiters or "spatter dashes." He totes a soldier's tin canteen and a haversack for his food. In his hand he carries a shepherd's crook.

6. The FARMER AND HIS WIFE wear simple, practical clothing. He wears a workingman's jacket, Osnaburg linen trousers and apron, and Indian moccasins. Over his shoulder is slung a small wooden keg of water. She wears a man's felt hat, a surtout, apron and skirt.

7. This SERVANT GIRL wears a scarf knotted about her head, a long checked kerchief over her shoulders (usually tucked into her apron) and a white linen or cotton apron over her dress. The dress, like that of most working women, is without hoops.

8. The SMITH wears a simple woolen cap, a checked linen shirt and a leather apron. His stock-ings are of worsted and he wears leather slippers. He files ironwork held in a vise.

9. The WAGGONER wears a frock, a long, smock-like shirt made of coarse canvas-like linen. A broad-brimmed felt hat protects his head from the weather. To protect his legs he wears "country boots"—strips of blanket tied below the knee and at the ankle.

10. The **COACHMAN** wears a watch coat over a single-breasted coat, a striped vest, leather breeches and heavy jackboots. His cocked hat is of the style worn by fashionable gentlemen.

11. The FRONTIERSMAN wears a fringed hunting shirt of linen or cloth over a homespun checked shirt. His leggings and moccasins are Indian style, and his breeches are of deer or moose skin. His shot bag is hung from a beaded Indian belt. His powder horn, fashioned from a cow's horn, is slung from a rawhide cord.

12. The CHIMNEY SWEEP AND BOY are in soiled and blackened work clothes. Their compact dress is designed for easy movement inside chimneys and fireplaces. They both carry long blanket-like dropcloths for catching soot. The sweep carries a sectioned broom which can be telescoped out to great length for cleaning chimneys, and from his belt hangs a canvas container for soot. The boy wears "mules" or slippers rather than shoes, and carries a short broom.

13. The COOPER wears a woolen or knitted cap, a checked vest and a leather apron. His cloth breeches are missing a knee buckle. About his neck he wears a kerchief, as did many workingmen.

14. This GENTLEMAN wearing a suit ornately bound with gold lace is headed for a very formal affair. He wears a powdered wig and carries a small sword. The whole outfit is a bit old-fashioned for its time.

15. The STREET PORTER earned his bread by carrying heavy burdens through the streets. He wears a cocked hat in the style of the 1750s. His old-fashioned tattered frock coat is a bit long for the period. On his legs he wears "country boots"—simple leggings made from lengths of old blanket tied at the ankle and below the knee. On his back is a carrying frame.

16. These UPPER-CLASS CHILDREN are casually dressed, as for play. The boy has taken off his coat and hat, and holds a cricket bat. He wears a linen shirt without ruffles, buckled shoes, and breeches that buckle below the knee. The little girl wears a simple summer dress with white linen ruffled cuffs and a straw hat with a ribbon.

17. The BARBER—like the tailor—was usually dressed in gentleman's clothing, but the cocked hat and coat on the one shown above are in the style of twenty years earlier. The bib of his apron is buttoned to his vest. In his pockets are scissors and a razor. A pewter shaving bowl is under his arm. In his left hand he carries a device for powdering wigs. He carries his comb in his wig while delivering another wig to a customer.

18. The MILKMAID wears a linen mob cap, a simple spotted bodice and a cotton blouse. Her apron is of coarse linen and her tattered homespun skirt has seen years of service.

19. The WATER CARRIER wears an old felt hat, cocked up in back. For warmth he has knotted a scarf about his head, covering his ears. His old coat has no collar; it is of the period of about 1745. His waistcoat has a speckled pattern. As did many poor people, he wears shoes that tie rather than buckle.

20. Both these CHAIRMEN wear heavy surtouts with capes made to button up and cover the wearer's face up to the eyes in bad weather. The man on the right wears a Scotch bonnet and offers his companion a pinch of snuff from his horn. The man on the left wears a linen stock or neckpiece, buckled at the back. Sedan chairs were the taxicabs of eighteenth-century cities of Europe and America.

21. The FASHIONABLE YOUNG MAN wears a bound cocked hat with silver cords, a cambric neck cloth, and a fine ruffled linen shirt. His spotted coat is known as a "frock." His vest is bound with silver lace. He wears two watches with tassled fobs descending below the skirts of his vest. His silk stockings have embroidered "clocks" from ankle to calf. His hair is powdered. He carries a cane but wears no sword (they were beginning to go out of fashion with young men at about this time).

22. The FOUNDRY WORKER wears a broad-brimmed hat which might be cocked up and caught to the crown with looping. His single-breasted frock coat reaches to just above his knees, and his linen or canvas apron reaches his shoes.

23. The GLASSBLOWER is dressed for work in a factory near furnaces producing great heat. His eye shield protects him against flying sparks. An ordinary coarse linen shirt and a smock-like apron falling down in front and back are his only garments apart from his buckled shoes.

24. The HOUSEWIFE wears a beribboned mob cap, a spotted bodice with a kerchief beneath, a striped apron and a heavy wool skirt. She carries a pail for fetching water.

25. This FASHIONABLE LADY is dressed for a grand affair such as a ball. Her lofty headdress is topped with a spangled turban mounted with ostrich feathers. She wears a silk polonaise gown with bows and flowers over a petticoat with a gauze flounce. In her hand she carries a fan.

26. The DOCTOR was immediately known by his full "physical" wig, his black suit and his gold-headed cane. His buttons and shoe buckles are of silver.

27. The **WHEELWRIGHT** wears a short jacket, round felt hat, leather breeches (tied at the knee, rather than buckled) and Indian moccasins. A leather apron is tied around his waist.

28. The town WATCHMAN was the eighteenth-century equivalent of the modern policeman on his beat. He wears a long watch coat, a single-breasted jacket bound at the waist by a leather belt, cloth breeches and worsted stockings. He carries a tin lantern and heavy oak stick. A clay pipe is stuck in his hatband. Over his shoulder on a cord hangs a "battle rattle," which gives off a loud clatter if swung vigorously, thereby summoning assistance in time of trouble.

29. The LADY IN RIDING DRESS wears what was then considered a rather masculine outfit. Her jacket is somewhat military in cut, with cuffs and silver-bound buttonholes. Her round felt hat is decorated with ribbons, rosettes and ostrich feathers. In her hand she carries a leather riding crop.

30. The TAILOR is dressed in the fashion of the upper classes whom he serves, with the exception of the workingman's kerchief around his neck. He wears a "snuff-colored" suit, and a small cocked hat. Around his neck he carries measuring tapes, and in his vest pocket a pair of scissors.

31. The MUSICIAN is dressed in an old-fashioned costume, even to his long, full-bodied wig. His full-sleeved coat and long-skirted vest are of the fashion of the 1740s. He wears a ruffled shirt and linen stock.

32. The KNIFE GRINDER, a street peddler, wears a battered castor hat, a checked neckerchief and an old-fashioned coat with buttonholes to the bottom edge. There were once buttons on his cuffs but they have long since disappeared. He wears homemade leggings of mattress ticking and a bibbed apron tied at the waist. On his feet he wears tattered Indian moccasins.

33. The GOLFING GENTLEMAN wears a distinctive costume designed to warn passersby (especially shepherds and herders in rural areas) that a game is in progress. This custom lasted almost a hundred years. His rather military-looking "coatee" is double-breasted in soldier fashion. His vest is of the short skirtless fashion becoming popular in the late 1770s. His fine linen shirt is generously ruffled at the breast and wrists.

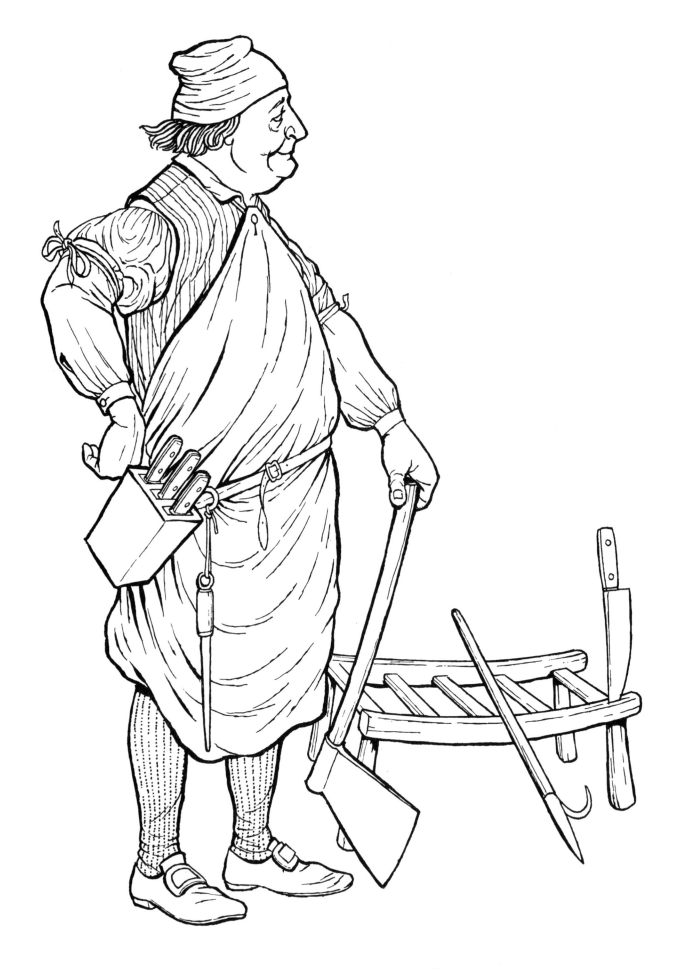

34. The BUTCHER wears a woolen cap, striped vest and a blue bibbed apron fastened at the neck. On his arms he wears removable protective sleeves to keep his shirt clean. About his waist he carries a wooden case of knives and a sharpening steel.

35. The LANTERN SELLER was another street peddler. He wears a surtout with a cape, and leggings similar to those of a soldier. Over his shoulder hangs a haversack for carrying some of his smaller lanterns.

36. The clothing of the QUAKER COUPLE tends to be somewhat old-fashioned for the period. He wears a surtout over his shoulders and a dark, sober suit of clothes. His round hat is not fashion- ably cocked up. His wife's dark and conservative gown is worn with a white bib and is modestly decorated with a flower.

37. The **FISHERMAN** wears a knitted Monmouth cap, a sailor's jacket and trousers, and heavy leather sea boots. His shirt is of coarse linen. He carries a boat hook and a heaving line.

38. The SHOPKEEPER wears a hat with cockades on three sides. His hair is curled and powdered, and his frock coat is typical of the 1770s. His apron is of green baize and his stockings are worsted.

39. The **FISHMONGER** of Boston wears a small round felt hat edged with white tape. His vest is double-breasted, and his short jacket is very simple, with no cuffs, lining or pockets. He wears red baize trousers and a canvas apron probably fashioned from old sail. He holds a wooden shovel for loading baskets of fish.

40. This CARPENTER, a free black man, wears typical workingman's dress—a cocked hat, a seaman-style jacket, and trousers. He wears no stockings and has laced shoes rather than the more fashionable buckled ones. He is leveling the surface of a board with a draw knife.

41. This HARPOONER is a Gay Head Indian, of Martha's Vineyard, Massachusetts—many members of the tribe served in the American whaling fleet. He wears a brightly colored kerchief bound about his head, a jacket buttoned to the neck, and wide petticoat trousers made of old sail canvas that come to just below the knee. He is barefoot, as he might be aboard ship or in a whaleboat in moderate weather. He carries a harpoon and a length of line.

42. The POST RIDER carried the mail between towns. He is dressed in the fashion of the English post rider of the same period, with a leather cap and a red surtout or watch coat. His breeches are leather and he wears heavy riding boots. In one hand he carries gloves; in the other the post horn for announcing his arrival in town. A large valise containing the mail is secured behind the saddle.

43. This well-equipped RURAL MILITIAMAN (5th Worcester County Regiment, Massachusetts) is dressed in the Sunday clothes of a small farmer. His coat, vest and trousers are of homespun, made and dyed by the women of the farm. His broad-brimmed hat is decorated with a sprig of pine and a cockade of ribbon. Hung from a military waist-belt is a tomahawk instead of a bayonet. He carries a homemade wooden canteen and a soldier's knapsack. His gun is an old-fashioned Hudson Valley fowler, not a military weapon. Slung over his left shoulder are a shot pouch and powder horn.

44. The TANNER wears a heavy leather apron over another apron of sheepskin, suspended from the shoulders and secured at the waist. The leather apron is also secured by a belt at the waist. Leather leg guards from knee to ankle protect him from the strong fluid called "ooze" and the vitriolic acid that were used for tanning hides. The tanner's hands were usually indelibly stained and colored by these fluids. He has one kerchief bound about his head and one about his neck. He works in shirt sleeves and vest.

45. The CHEROKEE INDIAN CHIEF wears a silver gorget and peace medal about his neck; he probably acquired both trinkets from the colonial authorities before the War. His scarlet blanket cloak and linen shirt are not of Indian manufacture, nor is the cloth from which his leggings are made.

These items were probably acquired in trade at the frontier trading post. His face is scarred in a design which identifies his tribe. He wears feathers in his hair and a striped tunic bound and secured at the waist with wampum belts. On his wrists he wears silver bracelets.

46. The WIGMAKER wears a gentleman's sleeved waistcoat of striped silk, a bibbed apron tied about his neck, buckled knee breeches, stockings and leather slippers. His ruffled shirt is of fine linen and, of course, he wears a powdered wig.